Jigsaw Pieces Make Pictures

Sophie Quinn

BookLeaf Publishing

Presentation by *BookLeaf Publishing*

Web: www.bookleafpub.com

E-mail: info@bookleafpub.com

ISBN: 9789357440677

First edition 2023

To my family and all of my friends,

ACKNOWLEDGEMENT

Thank you to everyone who has ever encourage me or supported me - love you guys!!

Thank you to Bookleaf Publishers and their writing competition as well for this opportunity!

Dandelions and New Beginnings

Dandelions
Carry wishes
As I
Carry memories,

Dandelions
Change,
As We
Fight for permeance;
It is futile.

Dandelions
Catch sunlight,
As I
Chase dreams.

Dandelions
Leave,
As We
Are transient.

Dandelions
Return,
As we
Begin Again.

Dandelions
Carry wishes,
My wishes,
My wishes on shooting stars,
My wishes of new beginnings,
Carried away,
Drifting in the wind,
Tangled up in the pappus
Of a dandelion.

Hopes, Intrinsically Tied to Endings

Their hopes,
Like a shooting star.
Hopes,
Floating on the breeze.
Stay for the ending,
(please),
It should be enough,
(let it be enough).

The Finality of Footnotes

I was born crying,
And sometimes I think I cried it all out then,
And dried up my tear ducts.
Or sometimes I think that just dictated the rest of my life.

I was born crying and sometimes I think I never will again.
I was born crying and sometimes I think I will never stop.

Tears punctuated with gasps.
Sobs with sniffles.
Breathing throughout it all.
Breath, the footnote of life, but the centre of my story.
The cornerstone of continued existence, but the struggle of my soul.
Let it out and breathe.
Tears roll
And chests rise and fall
And footnotes end.

I Love You On Purpose

Sometimes I love you is as good as a
conversation starter as hello
Sometimes I love you is as good at ending
conversations as good bye,
Sometimes it is more final too.
I love you in anger, annoyance, distaste
I love you in joy, happiness, care
I love you in life
I love you in death.
The words as easy as drawing breath,
Yet I still have to be reminded to breathe.
Would you live for me?
Would you take that next breath for me?
Love me in every breath,
Love me in every whisper, every heartbeat,
every life.
Tap, tap, tap:
I love you on repeat.

Impermanence is Written in Your Soul (A Snowman's Ode)

A creation from powder,
From the very air and life itself.
Such a form, such an existence, could never last long.
A predestined death. A failure of form.

My ending, a heavy weight pulling down my head,
My ending, settled on my shoulders, since my beginning,
My beginning in isolation,
Created by others, from scraps and dirt and twigs,
Something beautiful from the discards on the floor,
But they never stayed –
For, I am temporary and it would not do to get attached.

But I am not asking for your tears,
(Even with my self-pity and indulgence),
Not when I cannot even shed the water myself,

Even when my body is shrinking, soul,
non-existent
And I, alone, so alone.
Even now, when I am slowly dissolving into my
origins,
The materials of my pre-existence replacing my
body,
Leaving not even a scar on the land, on life itself
–
Leaving no proof I was here.
Sometimes I question it myself,
But tears are for the living, and that's something
I never was.

Return to Sender

Some are born noosed,
I reserve the right of choosing my own rope
Choking me in this form:
Letter after unanswered letter,
Returned, Unopened, an inevitable lack of reply.
The same red lines,
Running through my careful hand,
Slashing through my soul,
With this self torture, chosen and buried in.

The noose tightens;
Every shaped letter,
Every formed word,
Line after line.
Tightening, Tightening -
Nothing.

My brain cuts, legs swing.
And I gasp.
Tears falling down my face,
Sticking in my throat, my mouth dries;
I choke.

Tears - proof of continued existence,
Proof of life,

So I let them fall.
Tears - proof of life,
So you never will again.
I love you in all its finality:
Return to Sender,
Along the envelope,
Along my soul.

Ocean's Embrace

Do you think Icarus was scared?
Scared when he fell.
Do you think he cried, or screamed?
Or was he silent, shocked and shaking.

Icarus, a child for a second,
Now, a moral tale for eternity:
A reminder not to climb too high,
A reminder that everything falls-
Eventually.
A warning and a tale.

Falling to Poseidon;
Did the god watch,
Watch as a child fell to him,
Did he dig his claws into the boy,
Into his morality.

Or did he turn away,
As the dethroned boy fell,
Into the Ocean's Embrace,
Now a story told for generations.

Was he scared,
When he fell?

Do you think of Achilles' demise?
Ordained in fate,
Or orchestrated by ego and overconfidence;
Open backed sandals only a physical chink in
his armour,
Hubris, a mental one.

Do you wonder,
If he wore the sandals purposefully,
Aiming to join Patroclus in Hades,
A loss of self after a loss of life,
Is that our future-

Myths serve a purpose,
History is repeated,
And Achilles fell.

Another boy in another life,
This one descended from the sea,
Belonging to the Ocean's Embrace,
With its swift tides and many natures.

Do you wonder over Heracles?
His many deeds,
The gods' admirations -
Yet his demise at their hands,
At Hera's power.
Not final,

Mortality now absent,
Not able to fall anymore.

Do you wonder at the constellations,
Recounting myths and stories,
Heroes of old, plotted in the sky.

Yet, those not a constellation,
Those not a myth,
Real in their life,
Lost to history-
Did they suffer as tragically?
Are they at peace now-
Protected by their anonymity?

When we fall,
Mortal and Modern and Real,
Will we think of Icarus,
Of the boy with the golden wings?
Will we be left to the Ocean's Embrace,
Unable to be saved.
Or will we think of the future,
Those left behind,
Not from mythology,
Real and True?

Will we think of the future,
The past, the present,
And still fall?

Do you think Icarus was scared?
Scared when he fell.

Myths serve a purpose,
History is repeated,
And they all fell.

The Child and Her Bear

My eyes fixate on the bear,
Small, scraggly,
Sitting there, just sitting there,
Face up in a puddle,
Wet through,
As feet after feet – thousands of feet,
Walk over it again and again.
Left behind.

Sitting there lying in a puddle,
A puddle in a bomb crater,
A puddle that a child, 5,6,7,8, complained about
The water got in her sock they say,
She no longer minds.

Too young, still too young, always too young.
I turn away, leaving the bear, the child, the cries, the fleeing,
Having left years ago. Yet forced to again, again, again,
My recurring nightmare, personal hell, torture chamber.
That child and her left behind bear,
Sitting there, patient and wet and small,
Alone in a warzone,

A warzone on the ground, a warzone in my
head,
Leaving my mind there, for comfort, for
company,
For the child and her bear,
Together now, for eternity.

Sometimes: The Causalities Of My Sanity

Sometimes I'm worried about the war
Going on in my mind
Too many casualties
And too many losses.

Sometimes I fear if I can take it
At all, or at least a little.
But I have to,
Keep fighting, keep going.

Sometimes I don't recognise myself,
In this body,
A reflection in the mirror,
A stranger to itself.

Sometimes I worry for the aftershocks,
An earthquake rippling through,
For if I struggle to survive the war,
How will I survive facing you, facing them, facing it all,
How will I survive the end, the pain, the loss, the mourning:
The after mass, promising to be so terrible and so cruel.

Tears, Fear and Eulogies

Standing in a room full of strangers
Enduring their whispers and gazes
Lying, trying to pretend I know them
The door ajar, a pathway to a past life
And now I'm stuck here,
Writing an eulogy for the girl I once was.

Their words quintessential questions,
Queries of dreams and plans
Of a life long gone,
A reflection I no longer recognise
And now I'm sitting here,
Writing an eulogy for the girl I once knew.

Everywhere, everyone has moved on,
Futures no longer uncertain,
Doors opened and closed behind them,
The room empties;
And now I'm lingering here,
Writing an eulogy for the girl I once wanted to
be.

Their penultimate page turns,
Another book in the making,
I am left here crying on the floor,

Wondering who I am
And now I’m lying here,
Writing an eulogy for the girl I once dreamed of.

Standing amongst those strangers, once again
I blend in with their unknown faces,
The door firmly shut, a window open
So high above the ground, will I ever go back?
And now I’m stuck here,
Writing an eulogy for the girl I once was.

Threads Woven By Fate Make Lives

I could write a sonnet,
Four by four, attempted with planning.
Every line an ode with your name upon it,
Every word enchanting.

I could fill pages with poems,
Write a book on you,
Weaving our existence on our whims,
Creating a new world without a clue.

I never could fit perfectly,
Without changing my reality
For what is life without hyperbole
And hyperbole, a mask disguising the pain of
what would be.

I will fill your head with half-formed phrases,
My attempts at making a chain of daises.

Daisies will die like all else,
Morbidly, like taking final breaths,
Having drawn their last card,
Lying in a graveyard
Of withered heads and regrets.

Limericks often lie,
Often symbolic as if
Veiling the truth
Each word weaving a web

Melancholia is misread
Even in acrostics

Possibly a childish form,
Linking yourself back to that previous person
Eventually, you realise that's okay
As are we not made up of every person we have ever been
Simultaneously struggling for one identity
Escaping the pains of childhood and its ending, as a haiku ends too fast.

Battles in our minds,
Some lost, some won, some ongoing,
Our survival, victory.

Untethered Wolves

Not yet a woman,
Not still a child,
Just a girl,
A teenage girl -
So how would I be a child,
A child, so innocent,
A child, to be protected,
No.
I am to be thrown to the wolves
I am to be blamed for 'tempting them'.

Not yet a woman,
Not still a child,
Yet it feels like I am both,
Lost in transit,
Stuck in No-Mans-Land,
Drifting through this world.

Not yet a woman,
Not still a child,
In some ways,
I am free,
In others,
Tethered and restricted and jailed.

Not yet a woman,
Not still a child,
But always here.

Stories Spinning Pretty Perspectives

I was a hero,
Just no longer yours.
I was a villain,
Depending on perspective.
I saved and vanquished,
I fought and lost.
Stories spun,
A hope, a promise, a threat.
I was a hero,
A hero in all senses of the word,
I was a villain,
A villain in all understanding of the term.
I am a hero, still,
Just no longer yours.

Sardines

Silently,
So silent,
Afraid of the smallest noise,
The dark cloaks us,
Trapped in its shrouding embrace,
I search.

Alone and quiet,
Alone and determined,
The lights still off,
The quiet almost smothering,
I listen.

Eyes straining,
Heart pounding,
Feet gentle:
The floorboards creak.
A noise-
Smothered too late,
Not quite hidden.

Every muscle tense,
Every limb poised,
A predator in every act-
I pounce.

Now I join their silence,
Smothering laughter
As we hide
The dark comforting,
Protecting,
The others slowly join us-
Cramped as sardines,
We've won.

Billions: As They Did

Fingers gripping pens,
Tracing letters, etching words.
Feet treading trails,
Following footsteps, walking tracks.
Tongues and teeth forming phrases,
Making words, holding conversations.
Billions before us,
Writing these words, walking these trails,
conversing in familiarity.
Billions before us,
Watching these sunsets, plotting these stars,
swapping their stories.
Billions after us,
Tracing our lives, discovering the future,
listening to friends.
Billions after us,
Living their lives, following our paths, sharing
our stories.
Billions now, here,
Walking with us, talking to us, or maybe existing
separately, yet intertwined,
Always intertwined.
A thousand lives, a million shared experiences
The same sun,

Dawn and dusk spreading coloured light onto ruins,
As they did years ago,
When they were whole and new and grandiose.
The same stars,
Plotting constellations, carrying dreams,
As told stories in ancient times, as led the way for those before.

Nurses; Fighters, Lovers

I talk,
Chatting like its my only defence,
The nurses grip my hand,
Guide my eyes away,
Fortify my barriers,
Man the wall,
I keep talking.

The mouthpiece goes in,
Chatter ends,
Thoughts stop -
I panic.
Breathing evades me.

But a pressure on my hand,
A voice coaching me through,
The steady drum from the nurses-
I escape.

Their bodies,
Shields,
Their hands,
Lifelines,
Their minds,
Battlegrounds.

Moving to conceal screens,
Hide pain,
Carry me away.

Its over-
Legs shaking uncontrollably,
Not stopping.

Jokes and comfort,
Reassurance and distractions,
Blankets and instructions-
Their turn to chat.

Bad jokes turned brilliant on sedative,
And relief, hugs and goodbyes,
Well wishes,
Float me home.

Secret Language of Flowers

Lavender and snowdrops and red
chrysanthemums,
Devotion and hope and 'I love you's,
Belief in ourselves and the world,
Childhood and girlhood combined,
In such a sweet smelling bouquet, tinged with
red.

Narcissus and rudbeckia and pink carnations,
Female ambition and justice and a woman's
love,
I am a woman, I am a girl,
Flowers are pretty, but deadly,
And apparently symbolic of me.

I am the Amaranthus, hopeless not heartless,
You are the Gladiolus in the strength of
character,
Freesia for us, our friendship
And Campanula for my mother, my gratitude,
Maybe the Hyacinth, a god on his knees, the
poet himself,
Felled with loveliness and consistency, for my
sister,
An orange rose for my brother's energy,

And the Solidago, for the encouragement my
dad always gave me.

I could communicate only in flowers,
Pretty symbols, fitting for a woman,
Hidden meanings, my own language,
A bouquet for you, a bouquet for them,
One for us and one for me, a reminder.
My family, flowers, as pretty in their meaning,
As the recipients.

Yet for me, not hiding my so-called, flaws
I refuse to be shamed by,
Yellow carnations for my disdain,
And a sweet pea for my departure.
An orchid for you, a wish for longevity.

This secret language of flowers,
Of Lavender and snowdrops and red
chrysanthemums,
Devotion and hope and 'I love you's.

A Girl Called Donna

A girl called Donna
Fills the room with laughter,
Smiling and Warm,
Teas and Chocolate,
Blankets and stories,
Stories, where the hero always wins.

A woman called Donna,
Dressed to the nines,
Brandishing makeup like a weapon,
Wielding beauty as a mark of danger,
Marching, with danger coded into every step,
Step by step,
Strutting in those heels,
Continuing through the pain,
Masked and protected,
Shields up.

Donna,
Feet aching,
Face damp and rubbed red,
Clothes acting as armour
Swapped, for trackies,
Blankets, and hot chocolate,
Hands covered in ink,

Doodles and drawings and notes,
Reminders and messages
Sprawling across skin.

Donna,
A myth, a legend,
A threat.
Gloves, and heels and glamour.
Weapons and words and danger.

Donna,
Her reputation proceeds her.
The stories she tells,
More real than believed,
But the hero, her hero, is less clear cut.
Danger in every step,

Donna,
A story herself,
An innocent nickname,
The final syllables:

Belladonna -
A promise, a threat, an ending,
Your ending, written in her every stride.

Belladonna,
A myth all the more terrifying in its reality.

A girl called Donna - her reputation proceeds her.

If I Have A Daughter

If I have a daughter,
A girl born from me.
I will tell her
Of my own girlhood,
Of my own life.

She will know of the world,
Know to cry and laugh,
Her voice will be too loud,
Or too quiet, but still heard,
She will speak and be listened to.

If I have a daughter,
I will teach her to be strong,
Knowing that even if she shatters,
She will not break.

She will know
Of my mistakes and victories,
Be crafted from my adventure,
Excessive love,
Talking too loud,
Unapologetically shit singing,
She will be herself,
Shaped and supported by me.

I will warn her
Of following the smoke,
Finding the fire,
But have plasters and water,
Tea and a spare bed.

If I have a daughter,
She will know of the world,
Of the evils,
But not be scared;
She will hold her head high,
Unapologetic for her place in this world.

I will tell her
That no one is a hero,
Yet support her,
Hold up her cape,
When she tries to be,
For no one is a hero,
But together we can be a little heroic.

If I have a daughter,
She will be raised
Like my mum raised me,
Like my granny, impatient and crass, showed me to be,
Like my grandma, loving and kind, helped me see.

If I have a daughter,
She will have parts of people she'd never meet,
Part of a line of women:
Strong and fierce and protective,
Loving and kind and caring,
She'd just be.

Dancing with Strangers and Friends

Dancing and singing,
Shouting and laughing,
Music reverberating within my very heart,
Coursing through my body,
The floor, bouncing, from our dancing,
More jumping,
Feet hurting,
Loosing our voices,
But still shouting the words
Familiar to us all,
This moment shared between us all.
Body on body, too close,
Yet connected, thrilling,
Stifling in our togetherness,
But I wouldn't change it,
Not for the world.
We are here,
Here and now,
Voices too loud,
Bodies too close,
We are here, together;
Strangers and friends and those in between,
Reverberating within me.

In Another Universe

In another universe,
Maybe I'd be
Smarter, stronger,
A better version of me.

In another universe,
Maybe I'd be the hero,
Fearless and witty,
Bigger than zero.

In another universe,
Maybe I'd be the villain,
Only in people's minds,
Self-protection, never just killin'.

In this universe,
I know there's no such thing,
No villain, no hero, just me,
And maybe that's what I'm meant to be.

www.ingramcontent.com/pod-product-compliance
Lightning Source LLC
Chambersburg PA
CBHW051744130826
49812CB00033B/999
* 9 7 8 9 3 5 7 4 4 0 6 7 7 *